# God Helps David

by
Marjorie Palmer

Illustrated
by
Keith Neely

MOODY PRESS
CHICAGO

© 1983 by
Marjorie Palmer

All rights reserved.

**Library of Congress Cataloging in Publication Data**

Palmer, Marjorie
  God helps David.

  Summary: A young boy's faith in God helps him tend his father's sheep and overcome a giant.
  1. David, King of Israel—Juvenile literature.
  [1. David, King of Israel. 2. Bible stories—O.T.]
  I. Title.
  BS580.D3P284   1983     222'.4'0924   [B]        83-817
  ISBN 0-8024-0191-0

1 2 3 4 5 6 7 Printing/DB/Year 87 86 85 84 83

*Printed in the United States of America*

Moody Press, a ministry of the Moody Bible Institute, is designed for education, evangelization, and edification. If we may assist you in knowing more about Christ and the Christian life, please write us without obligation: Moody Press, c/o MLM, Chicago, Illinois 60610.

# David, the Shepherd Boy

David was a good boy. He loved God. God loved him, too.

David lived with his father and mother. He was a little boy. But David helped his father.

David took care of the sheep for his father.
There were little sheep, and there were big sheep. David took care of all the sheep. He loved them.
He was happy with the sheep.

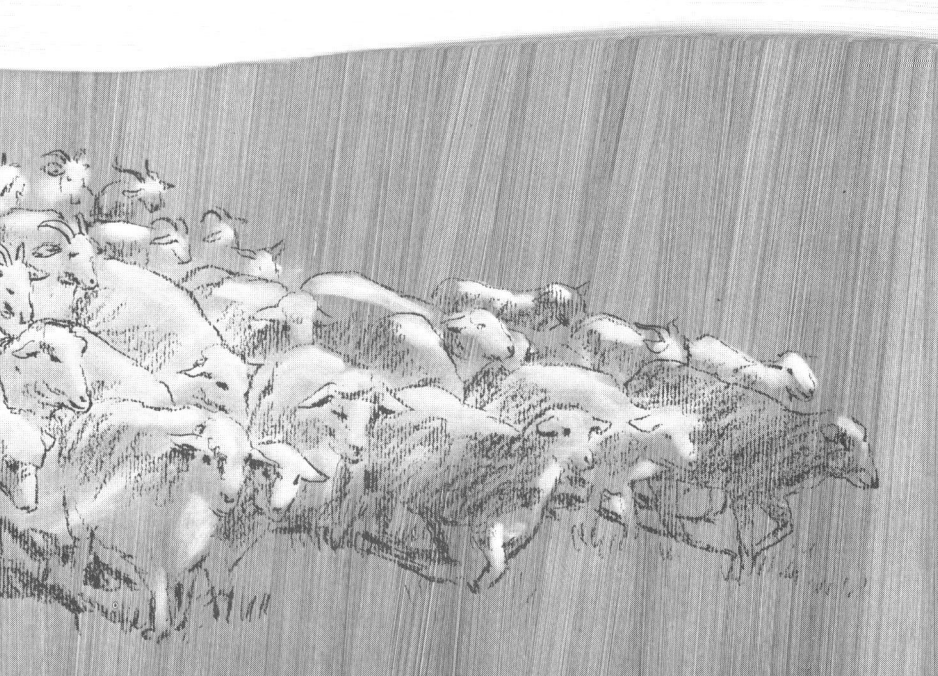

The sheep wanted something to eat. David took them to find some food. They ate the good grass.
David liked the birds and the blue sky. He liked the sun. He liked the sheep.
David was a good boy.

David took good care of his sheep. He liked to be a shepherd boy. A shepherd takes care of sheep.
David was happy. He sang to God.
David sang, "You are my God. You are good. I love you, God."

## David Sees a Bear

David went out with his sheep. Nobody was with David. He was all alone with his sheep.

David was not afraid. He said, "I know God will be with me. I am not afraid."

One day a big, big gray bear came. The bear wanted something to eat. He was a bad bear. He looked at the sheep.

"Oh," David said. "The bear is going to eat the sheep! Oh! Oh! What can I do?"

David knew that God loved him. He knew God wanted to help him. He said to the sheep, "Do not be afraid. God will make me strong!"

Do you know what little David did? He took a big, big stick.

He hit the big gray bear.

David killed the bad bear with his stick.

David said, "Thank You, God. I am happy the big, bad bear is gone. Now he cannot eat the sheep."

## David and the Lion

The sheep were eating the pretty green grass. David looked up. He saw something coming!

It was not a sheep. It was not a bear. It was big and yellow. It was a lion!

The big yellow lion took a little sheep in his mouth. The sheep was afraid. David heard the little sheep cry.

David ran after the lion. David was not afraid. He said, "God will help me. God will make me strong. I will help the little sheep."

So David took the little sheep from the big yellow lion's mouth. Then he killed the bad lion.

God loved David. God helped him. And David loved God, too. He said, "Thank You, God."

## David Sees His Brothers

David had seven brothers. David was the little brother. He had to help his father take care of the sheep. He had to work for his father.

But David was a happy boy. He loved his sheep. He loved to sing.

David was a good boy.

David had three brothers who did not live at home. They went to help the king.

David's father said, "Come here, David. I want you to do something for me. I want you to go and see your three brothers. Please take some food to your brothers."

David said, "Father, who will take care of the sheep?"

"I will take care of the sheep," his father said.

So David took the good food his mother had made. He went to see his brothers.

## The Bad Giant

David said to his brothers, "I am happy to see you. I have some food for you. Father and Mother sent it to you."

Then David and his brothers heard something. They heard a big, big man. He was a bad giant.

The giant called to everybody. He said, "Come and fight me. You are all afraid! Is there somebody who will come and fight me?"

The giant laughed at all the men.

David's brothers were afraid. They did not like the giant.

The giant laughed. He said, "You say you have a God who will take care of you. But you are all afraid! Who will come and fight me?"

David said to his brothers, "Why don't you fight the bad giant?"

They said, "He is too big! We cannot fight the giant. We are all afraid of him."

But David said, "God loves you. He will take care of you. Do not be afraid. Go and fight the giant."

David and his brothers looked up at the giant. He was dressed from his head to his feet in armor.

The giant was so big! But David was not afraid of him.

"Send someone to fight me," the giant said. "If he can kill me, the king and all his men will win. But if I kill him, all of our men and I will win the battle!"

No one wanted to fight the giant. They were all afraid of him.

Somebody went to the king. He said, "David, the shepherd boy, is not afraid to fight the giant."

So the king said, "Bring the boy to me. I want to talk with this David."

## David Goes to See the King

So David went to see the king.
The king looked at David. He did not look big enough to fight a giant.
The king said, "You are little. You cannot fight that big giant."

But David said, "When I was with the sheep, a bad bear came to eat them. God helped me. I killed the bear.

"And God helped me kill a big yellow lion," David said to the king. "I am not afraid. I will fight the giant."

"But you will be all alone," the king said.

"I will not be alone," David said. "God will be with me. He will help me."

The king did not know what to do. David was not afraid. But the giant was so big!

Then the king said, "You may go and fight the giant. God be with you, David."

The king took off his armor and put it all on David.

But it was too big for David. He could not walk. So David took off the armor.

David said, "I cannot go and fight the giant with all of this armor on. I do not know what to do with it."

David said, "Thank you," to the king. "Thank you for letting me go to fight the giant."

David was happy. He wanted to help the king. He said, "Thank You," to God.

# David Fights the Giant

David ran to the river. He picked up five stones. He put them in his little bag.

He picked up his shepherd stick.

He took his slingshot, and he walked out to meet the giant.

The giant saw David coming to fight him. He was angry.

"You are coming to hit me with a stick," he said. "Am I a little dog that you come to kill me with that?"

The giant came nearer.

"Come here," he said.

"You come to me with all your armor," David called back. "But I come to you with God's help. Now God will help me kill you. Then everybody will know how strong God is!"

When the giant came near, David ran to meet him. As he ran, he took a stone from his bag. He put the stone into his slingshot.

David whirled the sling over his head. Then he let it go.

The stone hit the bad giant on his head. Down went the giant. What a big noise he made when he fell!

All of the men who were with the giant ran away as fast as they could go. Now they were afraid.

But David's brothers and all the king's men were happy. They knew that God had helped David.

The king was happy, too.

"I want to talk to David," the king said.
So the men took David to the king.
The king asked David to stay with his men and be their leader.

David was happy. He knew God had been with him. He knew God had helped him kill the giant.
David said, "Thank You, God. Thank You for helping me."